Think Like a Scientist

COLLECT AND ANALYZE DATA

Julia J. Quinlan

Britannica®
Educational Publishing

IN ASSOCIATION WITH

ROSEN
EDUCATIONAL SERVICES

Published in 2019 by Britannica Educational Publishing (a trademark of Encyclopædia Britannica, Inc.) in association with The Rosen Publishing Group, Inc.
29 East 21st Street, New York, NY 10010

Distributed exclusively by Rosen Publishing.
To see additional Britannica Educational Publishing titles, go to rosenpublishing.com.

First Edition

Britannica Educational Publishing
J.E. Luebering: Executive Director, Core Editorial
Mary Rose McCudden: Editor, Britannica Student Encyclopedia

Rosen Publishing
Amelie von Zumbusch: Editor
Nelson Sá: Art Director
Brian Garvey: Series Designer
Tahara Anderson: Book Layout
Cindy Reiman: Photography Manager
Karen Huang: Photo Researcher

Library of Congress Cataloging-in-Publication Data

Names: Quinlan, Julia J., author.
Title: Collect and analyze data / Julia J. Quinlan.
Description: New York : Britannica Educational Publishing, in Association with Rosen Educational Services, 2019. | Series: Think like a scientist | Audience: Grades 3–6. | Includes bibliographical references and index.
Identifiers: LCCN 2017050388| ISBN 9781538302507 (library bound) | ISBN 9781538302514 (pbk.) | ISBN 9781538302521 (6 pack)
Subjects: LCSH: Science—Methodology—Juvenile literature.
Classification: LCC Q175.2 .Q85 2019 | DDC 507.2/1—dc23
LC record available at https://lccn.loc.gov/2017050388

Manufactured in the United States of America

Photo credits: Cover, p. 1 Ableimages/Photodisc/Thinkstock; p. 5 jamenpercy/Fotolia; pp. 6, 12 Encyclopædia Britannica; p. 7 Steve Debenport/E+/Getty Images; p. 10 Scott Bauer—Agricultural Research Service/U.S. Department of Agriculture; p. 11 Jenny E. Ross/Corbis Documentary/Getty Images; p. 13 © AP Images; p. 14 © Fernando Turmo/the Jane Goodall Institute; p. 16 Alfred Eisenstaedt/The LIFE Picture Collection/Getty Images; p. 17 Anthony Potter Collection/Archive Photos/Getty Images; p. 19 Science & Society Picture Library/Getty Images; p. 20 Penelope Breese/Hulton Archive/Getty Images; p. 21 Laura Doss/Corbis/Getty Images; p. 23 Steve Cole/amana images/Getty Images; p. 24 Elisabeth Schmitt/Moment/Getty Images; p. 25 krichie/Shutterstock.com; p. 27 Moving Moment/Shutterstock.com; p. 28 Hill Street Studios/Blend Images/Getty Images.

CONTENTS

CHAPTER 1

DISCOVERIES THROUGH DATA

There are many different types of science. Biology, chemistry, and physics are just a few examples. One thing all scientists have in common is curiosity. They all want to better understand our world and the universe we live in. They want to know why things are the way they are and what causes different **phenomena**. Scientists also look for solutions, like cures and vaccines for diseases. To do this, they need to collect data and analyze it. That means

VOCABULARY

Phenomena are observable facts or events.

The aurora borealis is a phenomenon that occurs in the northern skies. Scientists learned that it is caused by particles from the sun colliding with Earth's atmosphere.

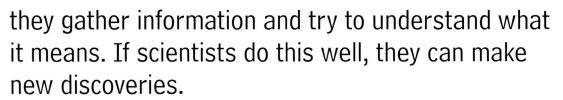

they gather information and try to understand what it means. If scientists do this well, they can make new discoveries.

To make new discoveries, scientists must go through several steps. These steps are called the scientific method. By using steps they all agree on, scientists can trust that the results are accurate.

The steps of the scientific method are: ask a question, do background research, construct a hypothesis, test the hypothesis with an

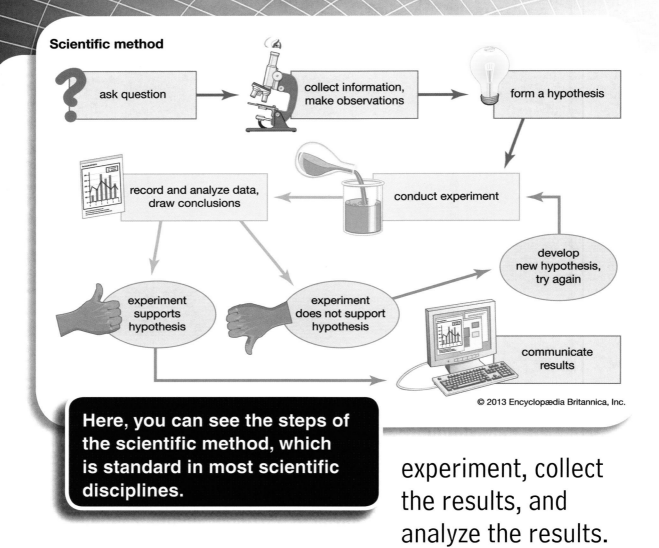

Scientific method

ask question → collect information, make observations → form a hypothesis

record and analyze data, draw conclusions ← conduct experiment

experiment supports hypothesis

experiment does not support hypothesis

develop new hypothesis, try again

communicate results

© 2013 Encyclopædia Britannica, Inc.

Here, you can see the steps of the scientific method, which is standard in most scientific disciplines.

experiment, collect the results, and analyze the results. The final step is to put the results, or data, into a report that scientists can share with the public and other scientists.

A hypothesis is what the scientist thinks the outcome of her experiment will be. Let's say that a doctor is testing a new type of treatment for the common cold. Her hypothesis may be that the new treatment will reduce coughing in her patients. To find out if this is true, she must conduct an experiment. She may give ten patients the new treatment. She then records the results. She may find that five patients coughed

Almost every person will get the common cold at some point in their life. Currently, there is no cure.

less and five coughed the same amount. That is her data. The doctor would then analyze the data and decide if her hypothesis was correct.

The data shows that only half of the doctor's patients coughed less. She has to decide that her data is inconclusive. That happens sometimes! She might try again the next day, giving the same patients a higher dosage of the same treatment. (That means she gives them a little bit more than she did the first time.) Or she might try the experiment again on ten new patients and record the new data. The point is that collecting data and analyzing it takes careful planning, careful observation, and careful recording.

COLLECTING INFORMATION

It takes time to design an experiment. Scientists must think about what they want to test and how to test it. They must also decide what data they are going to collect. To test average rainfall in an area, they would measure rainfall amounts. To find out how fast plants grow, they would measure the heights of plants.

There are many variables when collecting data. Things can go wrong or data may be harder to collect than you thought. Scientists must have reliable and accurate data when conducting an experiment. If they collect inaccurate data, they will have to start all over again. It is also important to have enough data. When scientists are studying the effects of climate change, they cannot look at just one town. They look all over the world and collect data. They may collect data on rising sea levels or warming temperatures. When testing something on such a large scale, scientists need a huge amount of data. If they do not collect

Collecting data comes in many forms. Here, a scientist collects samples from rice plants.

THINK ABOUT IT

If you wanted to find out what the sunniest day of the year was, how would you do that? How would you define sunny?

enough data, they are unable to come to a conclusion. This means they will have to go back and collect more data.

Sometimes scientists develop a hypothesis and collect data and then realize that their hypothesis was wrong. Maybe they did not conduct the experiment in the best way. Maybe they did not carefully record their data. Even failed experiments can

These scientists are measuring the thickness of ice covering the Arctic Ocean.

COMPARE & CONTRAST

Scientists collect data in many different environments. They collect data in labs, in forests, in the ocean, and even in space. How is collecting data in these different places similar? How is it different?

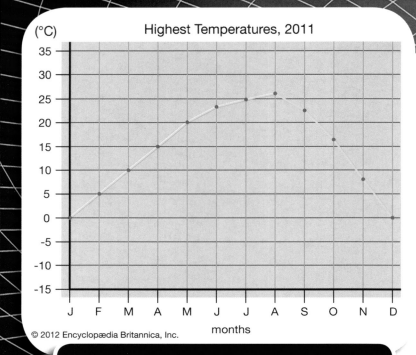

(°C)

Highest Temperatures, 2011

© 2012 Encyclopædia Britannica, Inc.

months

This line graph shows high temperatures over a year. To make it, someone measured the temperature every day and marked the highest temperature for each month.

help scientists learn from their mistakes.

Scientists try to collect a good amount of reliable data. Then they must analyze it, compile it, and organize it in a clear way that they can present to others. This can be done in charts, graphs, and reports. Scientists have to be sure the data they present to others is accurate and honest. Sometimes people can draw different conclusions depending on how data is presented.

Scientists are expected to present their findings as they are, even if it is not the result they wanted.

Many scientists work in laboratories, where they can perform experiments and gather data.

They have an **ethical** responsibility to present their data honestly. This can be tricky when scientists work for companies or institutions that want them to present only favorable results. A drug company might want their newest medicine to be approved and put on the market no matter what. It is up to scientists to test the drug and see if it works. If it does not work, they must be ethical and say so.

VOCABULARY

Ethical means following accepted rules of conduct and trying to be honest.

CHAPTER 3

THE METHOD IN ACTION

Collecting data can mean different things. Different kinds of scientists look for different kinds of data. One of the most famous **primatologists** is Jane Goodall. She spent years living among chimpanzees in Tanzania, in eastern Africa. Goodall

British scientist Jane Goodall is known for her research on chimpanzees. Her discoveries changed the way chimpanzees are studied and understood.

collected data about what chimpanzees ate and how they behaved.

Goodall observed chimpanzees make tools and use them for different things like gathering food. She found that they lived in complex social groups. Goodall discovered that chimpanzees were much more intelligent than people thought. Her discoveries were not easy to make. They came after many years of careful observation and data collection.

THINK ABOUT IT

Before Jane Goodall studied chimpanzees, people thought only humans could use tools. Would people have believed her if she had only seen one chimpanzee using tools?

One of the most famous scientific discoveries is penicillin. Penicillin is an **antibiotic** that can treat many different infections. A British doctor named

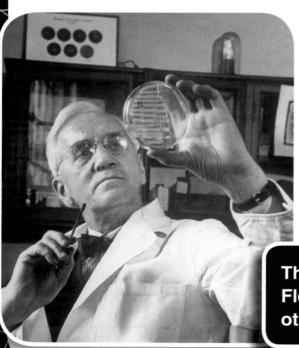

Alexander Fleming discovered penicillin in his lab by accident. In the summer of 1928, Fleming left out some containers that had harmful bacteria in them. When he came back to

The Scottish scientist Alexander Fleming discovered the first antibiotic drug, penicillin.

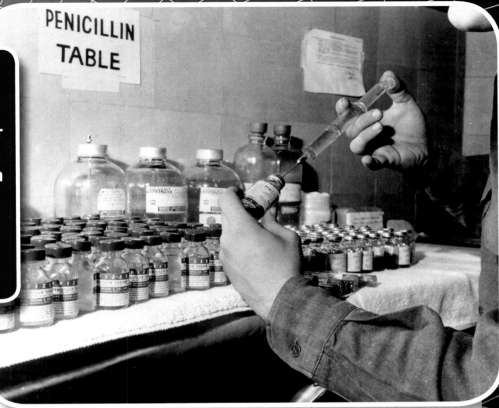

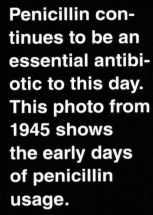
Penicillin continues to be an essential antibiotic to this day. This photo from 1945 shows the early days of penicillin usage.

them a few days later, he observed that some mold had grown in them. This new mold had stopped the growth of the harmful bacteria. It was a big discovery, but it had to be tested more before anyone knew what to do with it.

Another doctor named Howard Florey learned about Fleming's discovery. He thought he could use penicillin to cure diseases. Florey did his own experiments and collected the data. He gave penicillin to mice that were sick and found that the mice got better. A few years later, doctors started using penicillin on people. It was a great success!

Another great discovery was the tiny particle called an electron. An electron is one part of an atom. In 1898, a physicist named J. J. Thomson was experimenting with electricity inside of glass tubes. He observed some rays in the tubes that people did not understand. Thomson believed these rays were made of particles even smaller than atoms. His discovery did not come easily. He had many failures and experimented with many hypotheses. Thomson's work led many other scientists to try his experiments. They helped to prove his discovery of the electron.

British physicist J. J. Thomson discovered the particle called the electron. He received the Nobel Prize in Physics in 1906.

All of these scientists had to deal with many variables. Scientists have to keep variables in mind when they plan their experiments. That way they can compile the best data possible.

To collect data, Goodall spent time in the jungle observing chimpanzee behavior.

Some variables can be controlled for and others cannot. As you can guess, Jane Goodall did not have very much control over what the chimpanzees would do!

COMPARE & CONTRAST

How might Goodall's data have been similar to Fleming's? How would it have been different?

Many scientists work in labs that are completely sterile, or clean. This makes the data they collect more reliable.

Scientists often have to collect lots and lots of data. The scientists experimenting with penicillin had to be very thorough before they could risk testing it on people. All scientists have to analyze their data carefully. They must organize it in a way that others can understand. Data is just a jumble of information before it is analyzed.

CHAPTER 4

DATA IN OUR WORLD

Collecting and analyzing data is not just for scientists, doctors, and researchers. You can collect and analyze data, too! Start with something you are curious about, like the weather. Maybe you think that Monday always seems to be the coldest day of the week. That could be true or it could just feel that way. You can figure out if it's true by collecting and analyzing data. First, make sure you have a good outdoor thermometer to measure the air temperature. Then check the temperature on Monday and write it down. Do the same thing the next day. If you write down the temperature every day for a month, you will have a lot of data. You can then analyze the data by comparing the temperature on each Monday to the tempera- ture on the rest of the days of the week.

In your experiment, be sure to think about possible variables. For example, it is often colder in the morning and warmer in the afternoon. So, it would make sense to measure the temperature at the same time of day every day for that month.

It is important to plan your experiment and data collection in advance. This will make

There is data to collect all around us! Just from looking out the window you can find something to observe and analyze.

It is very important to carefully record your data. Double-check that you are entering data accurately and in the right location.

THINK ABOUT IT

What are other variables to think about when measuring temperatures? Does it matter where you place the thermometer each day?

it easier to perform your experiment. And it will make it easier to analyze your data at the end. Organize your information in columns. Label each column with a day of the week and write the temperature under it. Once you finish taking the temperature every day at the same time for a month, you can analyze your data and decide if your hypothesis was correct.

There are many things to observe in your own home. Have you ever noticed that if you leave bread out on the counter, after a while it will start to grow mold? All types of food will rot if they are left out long enough. But how long do different foods

What tools will you need for your experiment? An outdoor thermometer is important for taking accurate measurements.

How is an experiment to measure temperatures similar to an experiment to see how fast mold grows? How are they different?

take to grow mold? Which ones do you think grow mold the fastest?

There are many different types of bread. If they are left out, they will certainly grow mold. But, through careful observation, you can figure out which one gets mold the fastest.

You can design an experiment to try to determine this. As with the weather experiment, pick a time frame. Let's say one week. Also, be careful how you state your hypothesis. That way, you can be sure you are looking for the right data. If your hypothesis is that white bread will grow mold the fastest, do you mean it will get

Different types of bread are made with different ingredients. This can affect how quickly bread grows mold.

a spot of mold first or will become covered in mold the fastest? Once you state your hypothesis, you sometimes need to refine it.

Think about where you will place your bread. That is another variable. Would bread left in a

Making notes of your observations is key. It is always better to have too much information than too little!

sunny window grow mold faster than bread left in a cool, dark corner? To ensure good results, all of the bread must be placed in the same kind of environment. Check the bread and record your observations at the end of each day, or in the morning after you wake up. At the end of the week, you will be able to go over your observations and decide if the white bread grew mold the fastest.

By carefully collecting data, and always keeping variables in mind, you can analyze many things in everyday life. The scientific method can help us understand phenomena in our own lives. It also helps scientists understand the world around us.

GLOSSARY

atom One of the tiny particles that are the building blocks of all matter.

bacteria Small organisms, or living things, that can be found in all natural environments. They are made of a single cell.

biology A branch of knowledge that deals with living things and life processes.

chemistry A science that deals with the composition, structure, and properties of substances and the changes they go through.

climate The average weather conditions of a particular place or region over a period of years.

electricity The energy you get when tiny particles called electrons flow from place to place.

environment All the physical surroundings on Earth or in a particular place.

hypothesis An attempt to explain a problem; a statement that can be tested.

inconclusive Not leading to a definite conclusion or result.

infection Disease caused by germs.

physics A science that deals with matter and energy and their actions upon each other.

refine To improve by introducing something that makes a small difference.

treatment The act or manner or an instance of providing medical care for someone or something.

vaccine Substance that prevents the spread of disease that is based on the virus or bacteria that causes that disease.

variable A part of an experiment that can change.

FOR MORE INFORMATION

Carmichael, L. E. *The Scientific Method in the Real World.* North Mankato, MN: Core Publishing, 2013.

Flatt, Lizann. *Collecting Data* (Get Graphing! Building Data Literacy Skills). New York, NY: Crabtree Publishing Company, 2017.

Guzman, Sienna. *Visiting Death Valley: Represent and Interpret Data* (Math Masters: Measurement and Data). New York, NY: PowerKids Press, 2015.

Kniedel, Sally. *Creepy Crawlies and the Scientific Method: More Than 100 Hands-on Experiments for Children.* Golden, CO: Fulcrum Publishing, 2015.

Rosen, William. *Miracle Cure: The Creation of Antibiotics and the Birth of Modern Medicine.* New York, NY: Viking, 2017.

Silvey, Anita. *Untamed: The Wild Life of Jane Goodall.* Washington, DC: National Geographic Children's Books, 2015.

WEBSITES

Community Tool Box
http://ctb.ku.edu/en/table-of-contents/evaluate/evaluate-community -interventions/collect-analyze-data/main
Twitter: @CToolBox, Facebook: @CommunityToolBox

PBS Kids
http://pbskids.org/video/ready-jet-go/2365644213

Science Bob
https://sciencebob.com
Twitter, Facebook, Instagram: @ScienceBob

INDEX